IMAGES
of America

BULLOCH
COUNTY

♦ FAIR EDITION ♦

STATESBORO NEWS.

Vol. 8.   Statesboro, Ga., Friday, October 16, 1903.   No. 82.

CITY OF STATESBORO

BULLOCH COUNTY

BULLOCH COUNTY,
The Home of Sea Island Cotton; Produces One-Tenth of the Crop of the World.

STATESBORO,
The Biggest Inland Sea Island Cotton Market in the World. Handles One-Eighth of the Crop of the World.

This fair edition of the *Statesboro News* was published on Friday, October 16, 1903. Forty-eight pages in length, it was distributed to subscribers and, especially, to those who visited Bulloch County's agricultural exhibits at the Georgia State Fair held in Macon. In 1906 the county's exhibit won first place and was purchased by the State of Georgia to be presented at a national exposition in Jamestown, Virginia. The editor expansively described local accomplishments: "Just notice these: 100 varieties of hay, fifty varieties of wheat, as many of oats, sirups that appear as sweet as the memory of a first love affair; twelve varieties of sweet potatoes, varieties of hemp that grow on the earth, in the air or water under the earth, world without end, in Bulloch County, amen. . . . Vegetables from Chinese cabbage to common field peas and back again, and they are all included (watermelons, per-simmons, peaches, pears, apples, pumpkins . . .)."

IMAGES
of America

BULLOCH
COUNTY

Delma E. Presley and Smith C. Banks

ARCADIA
PUBLISHING

Published by Arcadia Publishing
Charleston, South Carolina

For all general information contact Arcadia Publishing at:
Telephone 843-853-2070
Fax 843-853-0044
E-mail sales@arcadiapublishing.com
For customer service and orders:
Toll-Free 1-888-313-2665

Visit us on the Internet at www.arcadiapublishing.com

Dedicated to:
Kemp Mabry
More than anyone in the twentieth century, he
has encouraged the preservation of Bulloch County's history.

Contents

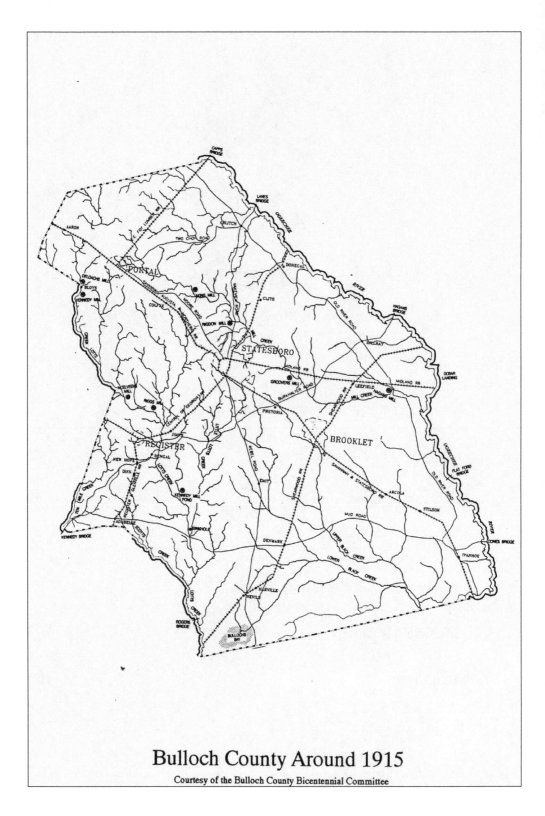

Bulloch County Around 1915

Courtesy of the Bulloch County Bicentennial Committee

Introduction

When Bulloch County was formed in 1796, it became one of the young state of Georgia's largest counties. Composed of over 500,000 acres of land, it was nearly the size of the state of Rhode Island. Bulloch gave up some of its territory when the neighboring counties of Emanuel, Jenkins, Candler, and Evans were formed. Today, it is the eighth largest of Georgia's 159 counties.

The earliest settlers sometimes called it the "State of Bulloch," with the Ogeechee River on the eastern border and the Canoochee on the west. They converted Native American paths into roads and named their county seat "Statesborough." Optimism and, perhaps, a sense of innate pride guided those whose family names are still easy to recognize two hundred years later: Alderman, Anderson, Banks, Bland, Brannen, Cone, DeLoach, Denmark, Everett, Fletcher, Franklin, Hagan, Hodges, Jernigan, Jones, Kennedy, Kirkland, Lanier, Lee, McCall, Mikell, Nevill, Olliff, Parrish, Rawls, Richardson, Roberts, Stanford, Tillman, Waters, Williams, and Wise. Their sons and daughters kept the faith, and their testimonial is a county called Bulloch—named for Archibald Bulloch, the president of the Executive Council of Georgia in 1776.

Bulloch's earliest settlers—herdsmen and small-time farmers—were a determined lot. They eagerly took on the arduous task of clearing the forests, building homesteads, and organizing churches and schools. Many of their ancestors had lived in Northern Ireland and England. Others traced their heritage to Scotland, Wales, France, Germany, and West Africa.

By 1860 there were only three thousand residents, more or less, in the county, and most of them lived near the Ogeechee River. It was not until after the War Between the States that Bulloch experienced its growth spurt. By 1880 the population had nearly tripled. What did this diverse citizenry have in common? Simply this: most believed they had settled on the best remaining piece of the good earth the nation had to offer.

If Bulloch initially did not offer ideal circumstances, at least it had attracted people who wanted to make the best of what they had found. As he surveyed the county in 1849, George White wrote in his comprehensive work *Statistics of Georgia*:

"The county is inhabited by an industrious and kind people. Although the lands which most of the citizens cultivate are poor, by dint of industry and economy, they manage to supply their wants which, however, are very few. Many rely, in a great degree, upon game, with which the county abounds, and the productions of their orchards. The Bulloch County farmer would get rich, while others would starve."

Land in the surrounding counties had similar characteristics, of course: sandy soil with patches of rich loam in bottomlands along hundreds of miles of rivers and streams. But land alone does not a county make, especially if it's Bulloch you're talking about. Georgia's famous poet, Sidney Lanier, captured the true heritage of Bulloch County when he wrote in 1869, "Thar's more in the man than thar is in the land." In this county the human factor has always spelled the difference between subsistence and success.

What the early families had, more than anything else, was an attitude. They wanted to succeed so much that they made "effort" a local tradition. Earlier in this century this slogan could be seen on letterheads and heard on the local radio station: "Bulloch County: where nature smiles and progress has the right of way."

No better example of Bulloch's single-minded determination can be found than this episode from the autumn of 1906. The State of Georgia announced that an agricultural and mechanical school would be established in the first congressional district. The school was to serve southeastern and coastal Georgia, and the new school would be awarded to the community which offered the highest bid. It was a prize sought by a number of counties in the region. Authorities scheduled the critical decision for December 1, 1906, at the DeSoto Hotel in Savannah. The local newspaper editor wrote the following headline: "Bulloch County Must Have That College." The editorial continued, "The feeling is unanimous for the committee to go down to Savannah . . . and simply get the college, that there shall be no limit to the amount that we shall pay for it, within reason."

On that momentous day in 1906, one hundred citizens boarded the train for Savannah and lobbied for the cause—an impressive demonstration of local support. As the day wore on, various contenders dropped out of the bidding. Finally, three remained: Emanuel, Tattnall, and Bulloch Counties. The top bids were from Tattnall and Bulloch. Both had pledged $95,000. Then the determined delegation from Bulloch held a caucus and decided to raise the stakes to $125,500. Their sweetened bid included a campus of 300 choice acres on the south side of Statesboro. The proud one hundred returned home with a contract for the First District A & M School, now known as Georgia Southern University. This major regional university enrolls over fourteen thousand students. Its proud motto, "Academic Excellence," also pays tribute to the spirit of those pioneers who would not settle for anything less than the best for Bulloch.

With amazing coincidence, newcomers to the county today often call attention to precisely those features which attracted settlers in the late 1700s. This is still a most appealing landscape of streams and ponds, of forests and fields. The economy today is driven by agriculture and the university, yet the local leaders have skillfully recruited and nourished industries which prosper in this progressive environment.

Recent arrivals are often surprised at how quickly long-term residents receive them into the community. This brand of hospitality stems from the county's humble beginnings. The historian White took note of this special quality in 1849; if he could return today, he would find many good reasons to describe Bulloch Countians as "industrious and kind." Our community has always honored people who roll up their sleeves and try to make the best of their talents. This book is a tribute to those people. As long as this spirit exists, Bulloch should continue to be the county that future generations will remember with pride.

One

Working the Land, Reaping the Harvest

In Bulloch County, the garden has long been a common bond within the family unit. Each family member plays a role in planting, weeding, harvesting, and preserving the bounty of the garden. Mrs. Annie L. Brown wears a bonnet as she digs sweet potatoes. The family cat observes the daily ritual.

W.A. "Bill" Waters, his family, and workers are pictured at his gristmill and sawmill, c.1910, in the Brooklet area. Mr. Waters, in the center, holds a grain measurer. Farmers brought their corn to the mill to be ground into grits, meal, and chicken feed. The miller took one-eighth of what he milled as payment for his work.

This photograph of John L. Johnson's Turpentine Still at Register, c. 1910, shows the distillery in the left foreground and barrels of turpentine stored on a platform in the center. Sixteen of Johnson's employees are shown here, including woods riders on horses and other hands, who are in and around the wagon.

This view of Howard Brothers Lumber Mill was taken in 1902. Located behind what is now a shopping center and near the present site of Howard Lumber Company, the mill relied on steam power and old-fashioned animal power provided by oxen. From left to right are: N.E. Howard, Judson Howard, Arthur Howard, Lewis Newsome, Mike Gundy, G.W. Howard, John Crawford, Dave Hutchinson, Mose Arington, John Clark, and William Howard.

William C. Graham, Statesboro's village blacksmith, served the needs of city and county residents. He began working as a blacksmith in 1918 and moved to Statesboro in 1928. As early as 1902, Statesboro was considered one of the largest mule markets in Georgia. Mr. Graham boasted of being able to shoe twelve to fifteen mules a day. When he retired in 1965, his shop was located at 11 Denmark Street.

Cotton harvesting required labor of farm hands of all ages. The crop was picked by hand, a most laborious task. Here we see a farm family in the cotton patch around 1910. From left to right are: (standing) Steve Miller and Mr. and Mrs. David "Son" Buie. The young nephews of the Buies rest on a pile of cotton at the end of a row.

In 1935, the Statesboro Ginnery was operated by Fred Smith and John H. Brannen. According to the *Statesboro News*, Bulloch County was the largest sea-island cotton-producing county in the world in 1903. Its 11,000 bales were over one-eighth of the crop world wide. On the left, loose cotton is being delivered to the gin, and in the center, a finished bale is loaded in the wagon.

Here, young Josh Smith Jr. of Westside "drives" a Moline tractor on the farm of his father, Joshua Smith Sr., in 1922. Crops on this farm included corn, cotton, wheat, velvet beans, peanuts, beans, fruits, and nuts. They produced all necessities except salt, refined sugar, and white flour for cakes and bread. Livestock and many kinds of fowl were abundant.

In 1902 Leland L. Foss received a patent for his double roller Sea Island ("Black Seed") Cotton Gin. It was said to do the work of two gins. Foss is shown here in 1936 with his invention. At that time, cotton was a minor crop in the county, but in 1914 the county produced 45,211 bales. Cotton remained a strong crop until the arrival of the boll weevil. By 1943 farmers did not plant a single acre of sea-island cotton in Bulloch County.

John H. Brannen replaces a plow point with the help of Will Devalle, c. 1935. About this time, he was named a "Master Farmer" of Bulloch County by *Progressive Farmer* magazine. Mr. Brannen used geese in his cotton fields to control weeds, and Mrs. Julia Brannen would pluck the geese and sell the down.

In this photograph taken by the *Atlanta Journal-Constitution*, John H. Brannen is shown with his hogs.

Hog-killing time was usually in November or December, when the weather was cold, because most people did not have refrigeration. In the right background is the cane mill for which a mule, harnessed to the pole, would provide power for grinding the sugar cane. The cane juice would be boiled down into an exceptionally tasty syrup. Pictured here are Outland Bohler and his helper, Rodney Johnson, c. 1940s.

In the late 1930s Bulloch County began the tradition of 4-H Club livestock shows. This large event in 1941 was held at Parker's Stock Yard, located on West Main Street near Blitch Street.

W. Lawton Brannen examines his tobacco crop in 1928, the year that the tobacco market opened in Statesboro. It was not until 1938 that the market had annual sales in excess of one million dollars. In 1965 the Bulloch County warehouses sold nearly nine million dollars of tobacco.

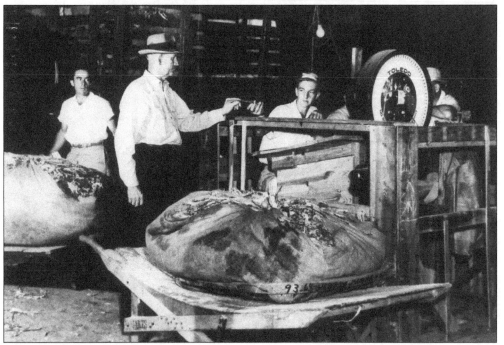

Mr. Wiley Mikell, center, oversaw the weighing of this sheet of tobacco at a warehouse in the 1950s. Robert Cox, far left, stands ready to weigh the next sheet.

One of the first tobacco warehouses in the county was operated in the early 1930s by W.E. Cobb Sr. and H.P. Foxhall, both North Carolinians. The Cobb and Foxhall Warehouse was located on the second block of South College Street. Farmers used automobiles, trucks, and mule-drawn wagons to transport the cured leaves to market.

Pictured at the first-day sale at the opening of the 1963 tobacco season at the Brannen Tobacco Warehouse are Aulbert J. Brannen Jr. (second from left), Aulbert J. Brannen Sr. (third from left), and Robert B. "Bob" Brannen (fourth from right). Behind the woman on the front row, to the right, is "Skip" Aldred, and behind Aulbert Brannen Sr. is his brother, H.L. "Pat" Brannen.

Henry Banks is shown as he oversees the unloading of silage (food for livestock) into a pit silo at Banks Dairy Farm, *c.* 1955. The storage pit preserved corn silage which cows would eat months, sometimes a year, later. Mr. Banks was named Bulloch County's Man of the Year in Soil Conservation for 1955.

Baling peanut hay in the 1940s on a Bulloch County farm was hard work. This crop provided livestock with both nutrition and roughage.

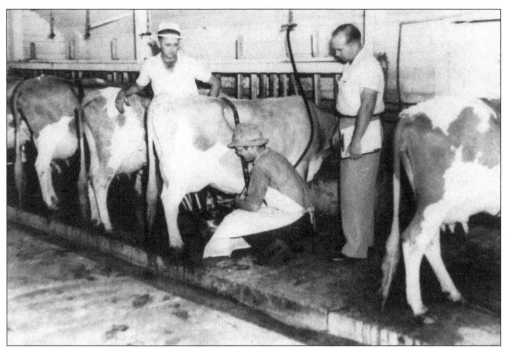

Health Inspector Thomas observed Wilbur Ward as he milked "Molly Moo" at Banks Dairy Farm in 1949. Standing on the left is Edwin Banks. The dairy farm was in operation from the 1920s until the 1980s.

The East Georgia Peanut Company was organized in 1945 by Homer Ray, S. Dew Groover, and Horace Z. Smith. One year later, the company built what everyone considered to be the tallest building in the county. The business is now owned by Gold Kist.

This is an aerial view, taken in the winter of 1950, of the Banks Dairy Farm in the Westside community. Note the silo, barns, outbuildings, and plowed fields in the left background. The two-story residence is the Brannen-Banks home, built in 1880 and remodeled in 1904.

Bulloch County prides itself in having more Master Farmers than any other county in the state of Georgia. This group photograph of honored farmers and their wives in 1954 includes, from left to right: (front row) Mr. and Mrs. John H. Brannen, Mr. and Mrs. Henry S. Blitch, and Mr. and Mrs. Cecil Gay; (back row) Mrs. W.C. Hodges Sr. with son, W.C. Hodges Jr., Mr. and Mrs. W.H. "Billy" Smith Sr. (the county's first Master Farmer), Mr. and Mrs. Delmas Rushing, Mr. and Mrs. Otis Holloway, and Mr. and Mrs. W.H. Smith Jr.

Two

Taking Care
of Business

In this view of East Main as it appeared in 1908 from the viewpoint of the center of town looking east, notice the famous walnut tree on the left and the Court House fence. The first building on the right is the Statesboro Mercantile Company. The streets were unpaved, and the sidewalks were made from boards. Note the fire plug at the corner on the right and the utility poles above the buildings.

The old walnut tree stood on the northeast corner of the intersection of the Main Streets in the center of Statesboro, just a few steps from the curbing around the Court House Square. This photograph of 1905 gives a view of West Main Street and of the Sea Island Bank, located on the corner of West Main and North Main. The cool and shady spot provided the site of the earliest court sessions, and officials posted notices there. It was also a convenient location to meet friends, conduct business, and gossip.

This view of South Main, looking north, was taken in 1908. Note that the wagons are loaded with bales of cotton that farmers have brought to town to sell to the cotton brokers. During the autumn market, brokers tagged the cotton and lined the streets with bales until the cotton could be shipped or stored.

Street Scene, Statesboro, Ga.

This 1905 photograph shows the first commercial block of North Main Street from a view looking north. The Sea Island Bank, shown in the photograph of the walnut tree on the preceding page, faced the Court House.

This rare view of an early automobile in a town of mules and wagons on North Main, across from the Court House (note fence), was taken in 1910. This is the same block of North Main shown above.

The Statesboro Buggy and Wagon Company, shown here c. 1905, was located on the corner of Courtland and North Main, opposite the Court House. Patrons enjoyed a covered sidewalk, but they endured muddy, unpaved streets in times of wet weather. Next door to the Buggy and Wagon Company was the Singer Sewing Machine Company.

The E.C. Oliver Store was located on the south side of East Main (site of the old Men and Boy's Store, next to Henry's.) In 1908 the store featured clothing and cloth goods. Tables of goods (bolts of cloth and men's clothing) were displayed on the sidewalk.

The R. Simmons Company, a popular mercantile store, was built on the corner of West and South Main streets in 1900. Owned by Rafe Simmons, a leading merchant in the region, it was the largest commercial establishment in Bulloch County. This general store accepted cash and provided credit. Mr. Simmons also bartered goods and brokered cotton.

South Side Grocery, located at 3 South Main Street, specialized in home delivery in 1910. The mule provided power for a smartly-equipped covered wagon, which also served as a moving advertisement.

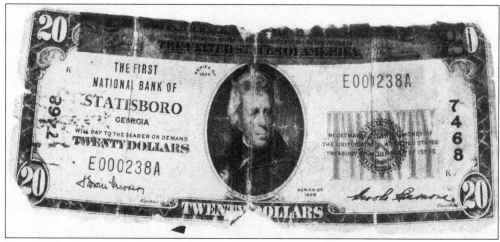

This $20 bank note was issued by the First National Bank of Statesboro, series 1928, and was signed by Brooks Simmons (president of the bank) and Edwin Groover (cashier).

In 1920, the First National Bank of Statesboro (side view) stood on the corner of West Main and North Main. This was an earlier location of the Sea Island Bank. This three-story structure was built in 1917. The Bulloch County Bank, organized after the Great Depression, was located in this building until it moved to its present site at the corner of North Main and Hill Streets.

In this view of the intersection of the Main Streets of downtown Statesboro around 1920, looking south, notice the marble block standing in the center of the intersection. The streets are paved. On the left is the Sea Island Bank, and on the far right is the three-story home of the First National Bank.

This view of East Main shows the Sea Island Bank and cars with placards advertising the Bulloch County Fair, which was slated for October of 1919.

The Bank of Statesboro, shown here c. 1920, was constructed in 1911 at a cost of $21,500. This striking building with an attractive facade still stands on the corner of Siebald and East Main. Established in 1894, it was the first bank in Bulloch County. Until this bank was built, farmers and merchants had to bank in Savannah or hide their cash. For a while this was the only bank in Statesboro to survive the financial crisis which began in 1929. When it finally was forced to close its doors in 1932, Statesboro temporarily was without the services of a bank. The Bank of Statesboro never reopened.

Several small shops and stores specialized in groceries and general merchandise on the north side of the second block of West Main Street in 1905.

The Rountree Hotel, shown here as it appeared in 1910, was located on the east side of the new Jaeckel Hotel. It was named for its owner, Judge J.W. Rountree, one-time mayor of Statesboro.

The Jaeckel Hotel was opened in 1905 on East Main Street by Gustave Jaeckel. A native of Berlin, Germany, previously had operated the business next door, which became the Rountree Hotel. The new Jaeckel was known for providing the best hotel accommodations in Bulloch County for over forty years. Many celebrities slept here, including Henry Ford, William Jennings Bryan, Cornelius Vanderbilt, and several governors of Georgia. It is now the Statesboro City Hall.

David Turner, right, was editor of *The Bulloch Times*. Here, he and his employees prepare the new printing press which arrived in 1908. Mr. Turner began his career in journalism in 1885. He was editor of the *Times* until the 1950s.

The Bulloch Drug Store in 1916 stood on South Main Street. From left to right are: Rupert Rackley, Paul Skelton, and an unidentified customer.

Lon Waters, the Watkins man, made home deliveries of remedies, extracts, spices, and toilet goods in 1910. At the end of the twentieth century, this company is still in business.

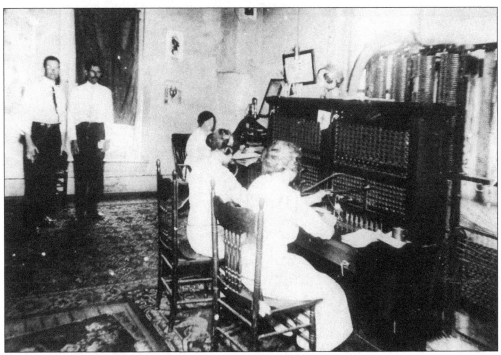

The Statesboro Telephone Company was photographed during its early years of operation c. 1918. The "central operators" are Bertha and Mamie Gould, the daughters of Mr. and Mrs. John C. Gould.

This is the Bulloch Packing Company ("Old Packing House") as it looked in full operation in late 1917. Packing House Road received its name from this company. Note the engine of the Central of Georgia freight train at the loading platform.

This interior view of the John Everett Grocery Store, located on North Main, was taken in 1923. The site previously had been known as City Grocery. Forty years later, it was the site of the Kenwin Store.

In this 1919 view of South Main looking south, the banner across the street advertises the annual Bulloch County Fair. In the right foreground is the R. Simmons Company.

Located in west Statesboro near the railroad, the Chero-Cola Bottling Company was in business from about 1900 until 1915. Another soft drink manufactured in Atlanta with the same initials was somewhat more successful. From left to right are: D.G. Edenfield, Joe S. Rouse, Watson Whitfield, Ira "Buster" Warren (at steering wheel), Homer Johns, Plunk Cross, Carl Blackburn, Ed Smith, and Mr. Weekly.

This photograph shows the bottling of milk in half-pint glass bottles at the City Dairy Company in 1950, located at 52 West Main Street. From left to right are: Cason A. Barlow, Lemuel Allen, Inspector Thomas, and owner Osborne C. Banks.

Here, Barbara (Mrs. E.Z.) Martin shows hams and sides of bacon to her children, Marilyn and Robert. Note the plump hams and sides of bacon hanging in the curing room at Robbin's Packing Company on its tenth anniversary open house in 1959.

In 1962, City Dairy Company, located on West Main Street, had a fleet of Divco vans for delivering milk to homes and stores in Bulloch and surrounding counties. From left to right are: Smith C. Banks (in van), Bernard Banks, and Osborne C. Banks.

In 1955, the Coca Cola Bottling Company held an open house in its facility on South Main Street. From left to right are (front row): Mrs. Grace Beasley (with daughter Emily), Mrs. Aubrey Pafford, Mr. Pafford (holding their son), and Coca Cola operator C.B. Cail.

The Rushing Hotel was located on South Main Street, the present site of the Statesboro Regional Library. It was originally Mr. John E. Rushing's family residence. He renovated it into a hotel in 1938. In the 1960s, it was known as the Georgian Hotel.

In 1947, U.S. Highway 301 was completed, and Statesboro began to call itself "The Tourist City," because it was located at the intersection of three major U.S. highways: 80, 25, and 301. Shortly thereafter, Mr. Will Woodcock built the Bon-Ette Motel, named for his wife and daughters, Bonnie and Willette. By 1966 Statesboro claimed to have eighteen motels, hotels, motor courts, and other facilities for tourists and travelers.

New, Ultra-Modern FRANKLIN'S DRIVE-IN RESTAURANT
At Intersection of U. S. Routes 301-25-80
STATESBORO, GA.

Mr. and Mrs. Joe Franklin opened Franklin's Drive-In Restaurant around 1950. Located at the intersection of U.S. Highways 301, 25, and 80, it offered restaurant service 24 hours a day. In the 1950s local young people preferred to stop here for snacks after late evening social events. For decades the restaurant cleverly has advertised "the world's worst apple pie."

Mrs. Bryant's Kitchen AAA
On U. S. Routes 301 and 25, Statesboro, Ga.

One of the favorite restaurants for travelers on U.S. 301 and 25 was Mrs. Bryant's Kitchen, located on South Main Street in "Andersonville," one block north of the entrance to Georgia Southern. It was noted for fine food, fresh vegetables, and a high rating by Duncan Hines. Many celebrities stopped at what they regarded as one of the best restaurants on Highway 301, which ran from Maine to Florida.

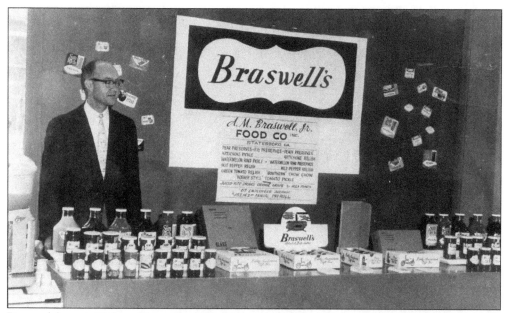

Pictured here is Belton Braswell, with a display of Braswell products in 1960. A.M. "Al" Braswell founded the A.M. Braswell Food Company, Inc., in 1946. His first products were watermelon rind preserves and pear preserves, and his first plant was in the old West Side School lunchroom.

Here, Jim Brock, manager of Statesboro Coca Cola, pours refreshments for guests at a Jaycee Industry Week event in the early 1960s. On the far left are radio station owner Don McDougald and Chamber of Commerce Director Al Gibson.

Three

A Time to Learn

Excelsior Academy, located in the pine grove of the town square, was organized in the 1870s by local citizens. The village of Excelsior, located on Ten Mile Creek a few miles from the Canoochee River, took its name from the Academy. Originally a Bulloch County community, it now is part of Candler County. The first newspaper in Bulloch County, *The Excelsior News*, began publication here in 1877.

In 1908, the Statesboro Normal Institute was located on the corner of South College and Grady Streets at the present site of the Statesboro Police Station. Trees planted in the schoolyard were named for members of the school board and other local citizens. Some of the trees survive today. The first building was completed in 1901. Additions in 1906 and 1913 provided more classrooms. The buildings burned in the 1960s.

Members of the 1905 graduating class of the Statesboro Normal Institute are shown here with friends. From left to right are: (seated) Myrtle Smith (Mrs. C.P. Olliff Sr.), unknown, and Gussie Lee; (standing) Carry Avant, Ruth Proctor (Mrs. Will Jones), two unidentified students, Agnes Blackburn, Jessie Mikell, and Annie Hedleston (Mrs. Milton Yarborough).

Members of the 1905 orchestra of the Statesboro Normal Institute posed on the porch in front of the school. The stringed instruments are guitars, mandolins, and violins.

This third grade class was photographed on the front steps of the porch of the Statesboro Grammar School in 1923. After the new high school building was erected behind the Institute in 1922, the old building became the Grammar School. Note the bare-foot boys in knee pants.

Shown here are the staff and student body of 1908 at the Tyson Grove School, located in Westside. The school master was David C. Banks, far right. Note the steeple on the building. The site can be found on the Nessmith Road on the Banks Dairy Farm. After Tyson Grove and other schools were consolidated with West Side School, the building was remodeled and used for the Tyson Grove Primitive Baptist Church.

The student body of the Martin School posed for this photo at the closing of the school year in 1908. The school was located in the Nevils community. Classes for grades 1–7 were held in a large central room. Younger students sat on the right side of the room and older students sat on the left. A wood-burning stove stood in the center of the room. The closing of the school was a special occasion in the community. The brush arbor in the background provided shade for the students and their families who attended the ceremonies.

The class of Ruth Hagin (Mrs. Bernie Lee Kennedy) at Brannen Institute performed a musical play at the closing of the school year in 1923. The school was located about halfway between Brooklet and Denmark on the Brooklet-Denmark Road. The children wore costumes made of brown and yellow pleated crepe paper. They unfurled their colorful wings as they sang this song:

"A little caterpillar in his cradle went to sleep.
He wrapped himself so snugly that you couldn't take a peek.
And when he threw the covers off, he'd make you say 'Oh my!'
For the little caterpillar was a gorgeous butterfly."

The Statesboro Industrial and High School, shown here around 1915, was located between Cotton Avenue and Blitch Street. To the right of the school building is a dormitory. William James came to Statesboro in 1907 to serve as the school's first principal. Soon it became an accredited and highly acclaimed school for black students.

Principal William James of the Statesboro Industrial and High School was elected an officer in the State Association of Negroes. Nationally respected and honored, he served as head of the school for twenty-eight years until his death in 1935. In tribute to the memory of Professor James, the school's name was changed to William James High School in 1948. In later years the school would become the present-day William James Middle School.

The William James School band, shown here c. 1950, was known for their excellent music and marching technique. They are pictured on the steps of the William James School after band practice. The high-stepping musicians were in demand for parades and performances.

The William James PTA, c. 1950, included leading members of the community. From left to right are: (front row) Henry Brown, Luetta Moore, Rosa Lee Chance, Amanda Smith, Sara Mildred Smith, and Zadie L. Douglas; (back row) G.M. Douglas, unidentified, Rev. W.D. Kent, Ruby Reeves, Carolyn Lewis, and Odessa Hall.

Statesboro High School was completed in 1922. The cost of construction was $46,265. It was located behind the Statesboro Grammar School on the south side of Grady Street between South College and Institute Street, the present site of the Statesboro Fire Department.

The cooking class for home economics students at Statesboro High School, 1927, is shown as they learn to make bread. Each student dressed in keeping with then-current sanitary regulations, including cloth hair coverings and full-length aprons.

A Statesboro High student clears the bar at a district track and field meet in the 1920s. This event attracted men and boys, who donned straw hats and driving caps. The pole and the bar were homemade of bamboo poles.

Pictured here is the Art Club of Statesboro High School, 1928. Miss Helen Collins, Miss Alla Walden, Miss Sara Blank, and Mrs. F.L. Floyd are joined by students Oliver Bland, Eugene Jones, Hazel Deal, Gilbert McLemore, Clayburn McLemore, Wright Everett, Constance Cone, Frances Parker, Elizabeth Deal, Claude Howard, and Earl Riggs.

The student body of Register School is shown in this photograph, taken about 1915. The school opened in 1904. The students ranged from elementary to high school age.

Register High School, a two-story brick building, was built in 1926. The school had been consolidated with the following schools: Atwood, Adabelle, Union, and Sylvester. Prominent in the foreground is Karlyn Watson.

Teachers at Register School in the 1940s posed for this photograph. From left to right are: Mamie Lou Anderson, Sally Blanche McElveen, Effie Gene Brown, Bessie Martin, Mildred Jones Brunson, Vera Johnson Bland, and Louise Pate.

Here, a group of children are pictured on the front steps of the West Side School in the 1930s. In or about 1929, Tyson Grove, Central, Smith-Allen-Deal, and Alderman Schools were consolidated into West Side School. It was located about 5 miles west of Statesboro on the old Statesboro-Swainsboro Road. It consisted of twelve classrooms, an office, a library, and a large auditorium. The cost of property, construction, and equipment in 1930 was $20,000. Note the children on the end of rows two and three making faces for the benefit of the camera.

Mrs. Lottie Futch's first grade class at Nevils School posed for the camera in 1945. In 1923 the Nevils School district voted unanimously to sell bonds to build the new Nevils School. The new school consolidated Reedy Branch, Martin School, and Bennet School.

The class of 1947 at Nevils School posed with their teacher Miss Jeanette DeLoach (far right). From left to right are (front row): Betty DeLoach, Elmer Byrd, Arminda Burnsed, Ray Hodges, and Catherine Anderson; (middle row) Emory Godbee, Vivian Nell NeSmith, Devaughn Roberts, and Sadie Newman; (back row) Loretta Anderson, Doris Davis, Jack Brannen, Louise Stalceys, Ronnie Durrence, Willie O'Neal Bragan, and Robert Rimes.

Here, students of Mrs. Olliff Boyd's kindergarten, the cast of a Tom Thumb Wedding, stand on the steps of the Statesboro Grammar School around 1943. From left to right are (front row): Sara Groover, James Albert Brannen (father of the bride), Ann Preston (mother of the bride), Laurel Tate Lanier, Sylvia Brunson, and Julie Simmons (flower girls), Patricia Redding (ring bearer), Pat Alderman (maid of honor), Al DeLoach (groom), Lucy Melton (bride), Pete Johnson (best man), Peggy Allen, John Pruitt, Jimmy Hagins (ring bearer), Faye Hagan, and Pat Lamb; (middle row) Kitty Kelly, Ann Lamb (bridesmaid), Peggy Herrington (bridesmaid), Kenny Bennett, Cecil Kennedy, and Sandra Pruitt; (back row) Honey Carpenter (flower girl), Tommy Cassedy, Lavinia Bryant (bridesmaid), Willette Woodcock (bridesmaid), Bill Nessmith, Linda Bean, Charles Clements, Nancy Sack, Coley Cassedy, and Evelyn Jones.

Mrs. Nattie Allen's fifth grade class presented an adaptation of the *Song of the South* in 1947 in the auditorium of the Statesboro Grammar School. Very popular with the community, the production had several repeat performances.

Miss Bertha Hagin's first grade class of the Statesboro Grammar School celebrated the end of the school year in 1943. Miss Hagins attended and graduated from the First District Agricultural and Mechanical School, which eventually became the present Georgia Southern University. She dedicated her life to teaching children in Bulloch County.

The same class, "The Original Club," returns to its first classroom—Miss Hagin's room—as seniors at Statesboro High School in 1954. From left to right are: Billy Bland, W.L. Cason, Charlie Joe Hollingsworth, Charlotte Blitch, Gene Newton, Jappy Akins, Jane Morris, Teresa Foy, Wayne Parrish, Guy Freeman, Sylvia Jones, Patricia Lanier, Lynn Smith, Jimmy Jones, Billy Jane Foss, Robert Waters, Ann Elizabeth Smith, June Carr, Shirley Akins, Smith Banks, and Betty McCormick.

Miss Myrtle Smith (later Mrs. C.P. Olliff Sr.) enjoyed a Sunday afternoon outing with Percy Averitt and his new horseless carriage in 1907. In the background is the new administration building and dormitory of the recently founded First District Agricultural and Mechanical School. The school opened officially on February 5, 1908, with a class of fifteen students and four faculty members. Miss Smith posed for Mr. Averitt, who took this photograph.

Mules powered the first A & M bus, which carried students to and from the business district of Statesboro.

Female students at First District A & M planted and maintained flower gardens as part of their tuition, as shown in this c. 1909 photograph. Male students learned how to grow basic crops such as peanuts, cotton, and garden vegetables, as well as animal husbandry. Female students took courses in domestic sciences, in addition to the required general curriculum. For many years the gardens and dairy provided food for the student body.

In the early 1930s, South Georgia Teachers College purchased a new bus which carried students to town and sports teams to out-of-town events. Miss Priscilla Prather (later Mrs. C.P. Olliff Jr.) is the young lady sitting on the left on the hood.

The last graduating class of First District A & M School is shown here in 1923. A year later the school became a junior college and was re-named the Georgia Normal School. Female students wore uniforms consisting of a white sailor's blouse with black neckerchief, black skirt, and stockings.

In 1935 Babe Ruth, having been traded by the New York Yankees to the Boston Braves, visited the area and participated in exhibition games with local athletes on the baseball team of the South Georgia Teachers College. From left to right are: Mr. Radcliff, "Gooseneck" Kettles, "Flicker" Wilson, Earl "Coonie" Riggs, and a young man named "Dub" Lovett.

On September 1, 1939, South Georgia Teachers College became Georgia Teachers College. This aerial view of the campus in the early 1940s shows farmlands adjoining the campus. It remained Georgia Teachers College until 1960, when it became Georgia Southern College. On July 1, 1990, Georgia Southern University was born.

The Blue Tide served as the bookstore, the snack bar, and the Collegeboro Post Office during the 1940s and 1950s. Students met here for relaxation and conversation. They could weigh themselves on the front porch for one penny.

Rat Week was held early in the fall quarter each year. Freshmen were required to wear their "rat caps." During Rat Week, each freshman wore clothes wrong-side-out and backwards. When an upperclassman shouted "Air Raid," co-eds were forced to "freeze" with their arms raised, and the men would "hit the dirt" (photograph c. 1950).

In 1962 the Georgia Southern College baseball team, under Coach J.I. Clements, won its first national championship by beating Portland State of Oregon in the final tournament game played in St. Joseph, Missouri. The team returned to the campus around midnight on June 12, 1962. A cavalcade of more than fifty cars filled with loyal fans met the team bus at Hopeulikit at the junction of U.S. Highways 25 and 80 and escorted the team to Hanner fieldhouse, where a huge crowd cheered the conquering champions.

In the early 1970s students at Georgia Southern College engaged in the fad of "streaking" which swept campuses nationwide. Although they immodestly uncovered their bodies, they concealed their heads with their drawers.

President Zach Henderson (1948–1968) initiated the tradition of serving watermelons to the student body and staff during summer sessions on Tuesdays and Thursdays. President Dale Lick (far left) invited Dr. Henderson to cut the first watermelon of a summer quarter in the late 1970s. Assisting Dr. Henderson is an alumnus, First District Congressman Ronald "Bo" Ginn (far right.)

Four

If Walls Could Speak

Here is the unfinished Bulloch County Court House as viewed from the west, facing North Main Street. Completed in 1894, this building stands on the same spot as the original log courthouse. The town of "Statesborough" was created by an act of the Georgia Legislature on December 19, 1803. The site was on 200 acres that had been donated two years earlier by George Sibbald. The county surveyor, Josiah Everett, laid out the town plan in 1806 and designated this spot for the courthouse square. The building was burned to the ground by Federal troops under the command of General William T. Sherman in 1864. After the war, a two-story frame building served as a courthouse. An act of the legislature gave "Statesboro" its first charter in 1866, and the current spelling thus began.

This bird's-eye view of the Court House and North Main Street from the top of the R. Simmons building was taken c. 1908. Note to the right of the water tank in the center is the Bulloch County Jail. The water tank indicates that city residents enjoyed running water and indoor plumbing. On the left is the tower of the Statesboro Missionary Baptist Church. In 1896, the Statesboro City Council passed an ordinance specifying that the main streets of Statesboro would be planted with water oak trees. Some of these trees remain today.

This photograph shows South Main Street and the city as viewed from the Court House steeple, c. 1908. Note the Statesboro Mercantile Company on the left (present site of the Sea Island Bank). In the left background is the tower of the Methodist church. The R. Simmons Company (later Minkovitz) is located on the right. In the background is the bell tower of the Statesboro Normal Institute.

The Confederate monument on the Court House Square was dedicated on Confederate Memorial Day, April 26, 1909. The United Daughters of the Confederacy raised over $2,000 for the impressive memorial. The marble sculpture of a Confederate soldier, standing at rest, is on the top of a 25-foot shaft of marble. Notice that a fence encircles the entire square. On the southern face of the monument is this inscription: "In the Memory of the Confederate Soldiers, 1861–1865." On another face of the monument is this inscription:

"How many a Glorious Name for us,
How many a Story of Fame for us,
They left: Would it
Not be a blame for us,
If their memories part
From our land and heart,
And a wrong to them
And a shame to us?"

This rare view of the south side of the Court House Square and the Confederate Monument was taken about 1910. Note the absence of columns on the building.

Automobiles parked parallel on the Court House Square in 1920. This view shows an expanded building, featuring porticos with Ionic columns which had been added in 1914.

This is a view of the Court House taken in the 1940s from the corner of East Main Street and Siebald Street.

This photograph shows the Court House as it appeared in the 1950s, viewed from North Main. While the exterior structure has not been modified significantly since then, the surface of the building has been painted several times. In addition, a major interior renovation took place in the 1960s.

Bulloch County's first post office was established in 1823 in "Statesborough." In 1918 this modern post office building was opened on the corner of South Main and East Vine Streets. When the post office moved to the Prince Preston Federal Building on North Main, the building was renovated and was used as the Statesboro City Hall from 1964 until 1996.

City Hall and Fire Department
Statesboro, Georgia

This view of Statesboro City Hall and Fire Department, located on the corner of Siebald and Courtland Streets, was taken in 1933. Two firetrucks are parked in the arched bays, and the City Hall entrance is located at the left rear. The calaboose (jail) was on the right side of the building.

In April 1959 the fire department purchased an American LaFrance 750-gallon-per-minute pumper. Shown here are members of the Statesboro Volunteer Fire Department. From left to right are (front row) Chief Bernon "Red" Gay, Carroll Cannon, and Claude McGlammery; (middle row) Ben Cassedy, Therell Ivey, Devo Durden, Earle Reaide, Emmett Scott, Reggie Beasley, Steve Newton, and Homer Lanier; (top row) Robert Helmuth and his German shepherd "Jet" (the mascot), Keith Howard, Charlie Shaw, and Billy Akins. Ernest Hagan stands at the cab door.

The Bulloch County Hospital was built in 1936 on the corner of East Grady and Donehoo Streets at a cost of $84,000. Walter Aldred was the architect.

In this view of South Zetterower Avenue from the corner of Savannah Avenue, taken in 1910, the wide street, unpaved, is flanked by newly planted oak trees. This was a newly developed residential area at the time.

This is the residence of David Poindexter Averitt, which he designed and built in 1886 on the northeast corner of Zetterower Avenue and Hill Street. Mr. Averitt moved to Statesboro from North Carolina and operated a sawmill in the vicinity.

The J.P. Williams mansion, built in 1906, stood on the corner of South Main and Bulloch Streets. A distinctive feature of the structure was its stunning beveled and leaded glass windows. Mr. Williams was a timber and railroad baron who built the house on the present site of the Trellis Inn Motel.

There were no churches in Statesboro in 1880. The First Baptist Church of Statesboro was an outgrowth of a Sunday school taught by the Reverend W.M. Cowart in 1882. On September 3, 1882, the First Baptist Church was established by former members of the Macedonia Baptist Church. Three wooden churches were built and destroyed before this brick sanctuary was erected in 1902 on North Main Street. The present First Baptist Church is located on this same site.

In 1908, the North Main Street residential area featured picket fences, dirt streets and sidewalks, hitching posts, and water oak trees.

The First Methodist Church of Statesboro was established in 1886. The newly completed building in this 1903 photograph stood at the church's present site. The church was known for its outstanding stained-glass windows. The gate in the foreground is the entrance to the property of the Statesboro Masonic Lodge.

Built by Dr. M.M. "Mat" Holland in the 1890s, the house on South Main Street across from the old post office/city hall has been called the Grande Dame of Statesboro. This Victorian structure with elaborate wood trim, cupola, and dormers reflects prosperous days in Statesboro at the end of the nineteenth century. The home is still standing.

The J.G. Blitch house was built around 1906 on North Main Street, across from the First Baptist Church. Mr. Blitch was a prominent businessman who ran a general merchandise store on Main Street.

The first Presbyterian church was established in 1891 near Riggs Mill (now Cypress Lake). It was organized as Statesboro Presbyterian Church in 1896. The picture shows the church as it looked when it was on the east side of Broad Street in Statesboro. This building was destroyed by fire in 1940.

The Statesboro Primitive Baptist Church was established in 1891 by Elder M.F. Stubbs, Trustees John F. Brannen, R. Simmons, Israel Smith, and others. Pictured here as it looked in 1898, the church was located on the west side of Broad Street at the corner of East Grady Street.

Macedonia Baptist Church is located about one and one-half miles inland from the Old River Road, near the Williams Landing in the Hagin District. The lumber used to build the church in 1854 was sawn in Emanuel County and floated down the Ogeechee River. The monument in the foreground commemorates the founding minister, the Rev. James R. Miller.

70

The First African Baptist Church was established in 1889. At that time it was called Hall Baptist Church. Its name was changed in 1900 when the congregation relocated to 24 Cotton Avenue. Here, it is pictured as it looked around 1960.

Union Methodist Church, founded in August 1790, is the oldest Methodist church in Bulloch County and one of the oldest continually active Methodist churches in Georgia. It is located on the Old River Road in the Blitch community.

Bethlehem Primitive Baptist Church, organized in 1841 by members of the Upper and Lower Lotts Creek Primitive Baptist Churches, is located about 3 miles west of Statesboro on the Westside Road, near the Watering Hole Branch. This building was built around 1900.

Upper Lotts Creek Primitive Baptist Church is shown as it looked in the 1930s. The church, originally known as Parrish's Meeting House, was constituted in 1831. It is located on the east bank of Big Lotts Creek near the Candler County line.

New Hope Methodist Church was
established in 1804 in the Hagin
District at what was later known as
Mill Ray. Here the congregation is
shown at the dedication of the new
church building on May 31, 1908.
The building cost $2,000.

The Portal Methodist Church is
shows as it appeared in the 1960s. In
1909, the town was laid out on the
tracks of the Savannah, Augusta, and
Northern Railroad. J.A. Brannen
and Hinton Booth held an auction
to sell lots for the town, and they
provided land for the Methodist
church, which was built around 1910.

Friendship Baptist Church, located a few miles south of Stilson, was organized in the 1880s by the Rev. Inman Bryant and Brother Tom Lonon. Originally, it was a brush arbor church. Mrs. Anna S. Groover gave the land on which the church was built.

DeLoach's Primitive Baptist Church is located in the lower end of the county near Lotts Creek and the Canoochee River. William and John DeLoach donated the land for the church, which was constituted in 1840. The present church building was built in 1872 on the site of the original structure.

Bethlehem Baptist Church is located near Register. In 1908 a group of members of New Hope Missionary Baptist Church withdrew from New Hope and formed the new church. The building is located near New Hope Church. It was used in the movie *The Greatest Gift*, starring Glenn Ford, which was filmed in nearby Register in the 1970s.

The Missionary Baptist Church of Register, shown here as it looked after it was erected in 1908, was located on land donated by Franklin P. Register, the town's namesake. The original cost of the church was $2,500. The building has since burned down.

Lower Lotts Creek Primitive Baptist Church was constituted in 1801 by Elders William Cone and Henry Cook. It is located off Highway 46 near the intersection with U.S. 301, in the old Bengal community. It is the second oldest Primitive Baptist church in the county (after Nevils Creek, which was founded in 1790.)

St. Matthews Catholic Church was established in 1934. The original congregation met in a house on South Main Street at the present site of the Stiles Motel. The building shown here, located on Northside Drive East, was dedicated in February 1950. This building was razed when the congregation built a new church located on Gentilly Road.

Five

Interesting Places, Memorable People

In 1901 Brooklet was the name for the new post office at Parker & Cone's Store, 9 miles below Statesboro on the Savannah and Statesboro Railroad. J.V. Lee was the postmaster. This picture of the Brooklet Baptist Church, organized in 1907, was taken on Lane Street looking east.

This view of Lane Street looking toward the west shows the Brooklet Baptist Church on the left as one stands in the center of Parker Avenue in Brooklet. Lane Street was named for the first mayor, Dr. John I. Lane, and Parker Avenue was named for W.C. Parker. Note the "horseless carriage" and pleasant shade trees.

This 1916 view of Parker Avenue (Main Street) in Brooklet, looking south, shows Robertson's Store on the right. This is the site of the Brooklet Post Office in the late 1990s. The house at the end of the street is the A.J. Lee home.

A view of the east side of Parker Avenue, *c.* 1916, includes the J.N. Shearouse home and the Dr. J.M. McElveen home.

This photograph of the railroad crossing at Stilson was part of the visual directions provided for automobile racers in the Savannah-Atlanta Auto Endurance race in 1909. The Stilson school building, with its prominent steeple, stands in the background.

Here, the Shearwood Railroad crosses the Ogeechee River at flood stage around 1910. The coaches carried people on a picnic outing. An owner, Mr. J.N. Shearouse, stands second from the left. The train crossed the river from Egypt, in Effingham County, and ran to Claxton, in Evans County by way of these Bulloch County stations: Bassett, Leefield, Brooklet, Watersville, Denmark, Nevils, and Edna.

The old wooden bridge across the Ogeechee River at Dover had a passing lane. The bridge was replaced in 1946 by the U.S. 301 concrete bridge.

The Savannah and Statesboro Railroad engines 6 and 7 stand in the Statesboro station in 1900. Note that their tenders are loaded with wood in order to keep the engines filled with steam for pulling long loads of cars to Savannah. The track ran from Statesboro to Cuyler in Bryan County, where it connected with the Seaboard Line and continued directly to Savannah.

This photograph of the depot and Bird Block in downtown Metter was taken around 1912. Until Candler County was created in 1914, Metter was the second largest town in Bulloch County. It is located 20 miles southwest of Statesboro.

In this 1901 photograph of Main Street at the railroad crossing in Register, the building at the extreme left is the Knights of Pythias hall. The railroad depot is at the extreme right. The two-story building is said to have been the C.T. Baughn mercantile business, which was destroyed by fire in 1915. Founded in 1894, the town was located at the intersection of the Register and Glennville Railroad and the Dover to Dublin branch of the Central of Georgia Railroad.

This is the home of Franklin Pierce Register, on the right side of Main Street of Register, looking north. Mr. Register arrived in Bulloch County in 1884. He established a large naval stores operation and ran a general mercantile business. The town named for him is located 9 miles west of Statesboro.

Burglars used dynamite to open the safe of the Farmers State Bank in Register at 2 am on October 7, 1912. Two young men stole $900 in cash, but they were caught and arrested ten hours later.

Dessie Waters, from the Brooklet area, was photographed with his mule and buggy in 1910.

The Pulaski High School served Bulloch County residents in the Club House District until Candler County was formed in 1914. When the Central of Georgia completed the Burton and Pineora Railroad to Statesboro in 1901, several new towns sprang to life along the tracks. The new towns included Parrish and Pulaski.

Portal, incorporated in 1914, was located on the railroad. This photograph of buildings on the north side of U.S. Highway 80 was taken in the 1960s.

Mr. and Mrs. Zachary Taylor Deloach built this home in Portal after they moved from their home near Bloys. Later it was the home of their daughter, Mrs. Mabel Deloach Saunders. The photograph was taken in the 1930s.

Engine number 209 was photographed on the tracks at Portal Station in 1939.

After the walnut tree was removed in 1917, the local government was able to pave downtown streets in 1918–1919. A modern steam roller made the job go swiftly.

The Bulloch County Bank was located on the northwest corner of the intersection of the Main Streets of Statesboro in 1940. This is the same building that had been occupied earlier by the First National Bank of Statesboro.

The photograph shows Bulloch County Court House, facing North Main Street, as it looked around 1905. In 1914 the county spent $12,000 on a renovation project which added four rooms on the ground floor, remodeled the second floor, created a partial third floor, and added a classical portico and Ionic columns on three sides.

The Central of Georgia railroad station was located on East Main Street. The Alfred Dorman Company, a major wholesale grocer in southeast Georgia, was next door (photograph c. 1950).

This image of Private Robert W. DeLoach, son of John Calvin DeLoach, was reproduced from a tintype photograph. DeLoach enlisted as a private in the Bulloch Troops, Company E, 5th Georgia Cavalry, Confederate States of America, in October 1861. He surrendered with General Joseph Johnston in 1865. Deloach later became a farmer and served as Bulloch County's representative to the General Assembly from 1873 to 1877. He was also postmaster of Bloys, which was named for his son, Robert Bloys DeLoach.

Private Ichabod Newsome enlisted in the Bulloch Troops, Company E, 5th Georgia Cavalry, Confederate States of America, in October 1861. He lived in the Macedonia community, where he died in 1894.

This photograph shows Confederate veteran William Richard Whitaker, active member of the Bulloch County chapter of the United Confederate Veterans, former member of Company F "Wilkinson Rifles," 3rd Regiment, Georgia Volunteer Infantry, Confederate States of America. Whitaker moved to Bulloch County in 1895 and lived in the Blitch community. Note that he is wearing medals and decorations collected at Confederate veterans conventions, including the Southern Cross of Honor awarded by the United Daughters of the Confederacy.

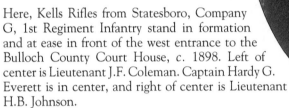

Here, Kells Rifles from Statesboro, Company G, 1st Regiment Infantry stand in formation and at ease in front of the west entrance to the Bulloch County Court House, c. 1898. Left of center is Lieutenant J.F. Coleman. Captain Hardy G. Everett is in center, and right of center is Lieutenant H.B. Johnson.

First District A & M students, including young soldiers from the school, participated in a statewide literary meet in Athens in 1917. Bertha Hagin of Bulloch County stands in the right foreground. Soon the young men would be sent away to defend the country in the First World War.

The local headquarters detachment of the Georgia National Guard unit stood at attention in front of the Sea Island Bank on East Main Street in September 1927. Col. Leroy Cowart, Commander, stands at the head of the formation. From left to right are: Thad J. Morris, Ernest E. Brannen, Charlie L. Howard, Jack DeLoach, James P. Waters, William Morgan Hagins Jr., Reppard DeLoach, Floyd A. Akins, Homer B. Melton, George C. Hagins (in back of Cowart), Albert M. Smith, Harville C. Ozburn, Denver Riggs, Harvey Brannen, Sidney L. Lanier, George Pete Donaldson, Leon Durden, J.P. Anderson, and James B. Averitt.

Members of Battery A of the 264th Coastal Artillery, Georgia National Guard, located in Statesboro, are pictured here. At the time of the photograph, May 1, 1939, the troops were commanded by Captain James B. Averitt. From left to right are: (front row) Rimes, Wynn, Barlow, Gillespie, Underwood, and Fields; (middle row) Robertson, Riggs, Robinson, Barlow, Brown, Boyd, Hendrix, and Hodges; (back row) Henderson, Barnes, Donaldson, Carter, Gay, Ellis, Deal, and Bailey.

Pictured here are other members of Battery A of the 264th Coastal Artillery, Georgia National Guard. From left to right are: (front row) Hagins, Brack, Parrish, Cromartie, Gillespie, Neville, and Alderman; (middle row) Strange, Scott, Motes, Gay, Riggs, Hendrix, Hall, and Creasy; (back row) Adams, Barlow, Waters, Edenfield, Hagans, Heath, Gould, and Youngblood.

Mrs. Susan Matilda Lindsey (far left) celebrated her 93rd birthday in 1919 at her home at Clito. Note her four-year-old great grandson, Jessie Quattlebaum (far right.) She and her family moved to Bulloch County in the late 1800s from Wilkinson County, Georgia.

The David C. Anderson clan were photographed in the Sink Hole district, *c.* 1892. On the porch in the background, center, are Mr. and Mrs. David C. Anderson, surrounded by their children's families. Note that the house was originally a log structure.

Shown here is the Remer Alderman "Add-on-House," or "Train House," located near Wolf Pen Branch in Westside. Begun in 1881, it was finished sometime after 1900. It is a collection of four houses connected by porches and covered bridges. The house grew as the family grew.

This is a 1930s view of the John Calvin DeLoach house, located near DeLoach's Primitive Baptist Church, south of Nevils. The house was built in the 1840s and stood until the late 1970s. This one-story raised cottage was one of the finest examples of antebellum architecture in Bulloch County.

Here, Charles W. Zetterower and family are pictured at their home in 1893, near Denmark. The house, called "Old Happy," was built in 1875–1885. From left to right are: Sallie (namesake of Sallie Zetterower Elementary School), Lillie, Mrs. Lizzie Roach Zetterower (with baby, Josiah), Frank, Mr. Zetterower, Lonnie, Janie, C.A., and Lemuel.

Judge Samuel L. Harville, seated on left, one of Bulloch County's signers of the Ordinance of Secession in 1861, was a captain in the Confederate Army. He is shown here with son Keebler Harville and family, *c.* 1896. Note: the one-story house in the background is on the same site of the present-day Harville House on Harville Road.

The Keebler Harville family is shown at the site also seen in the the above photograph, *c.* 1915. The old house was incorporated into the larger two-story house during a renovation in 1904.

Four generations of the family of Mr. and Mrs. James Gross Brannen posed in front of their house, located on what is now Banks Dairy Road, *c.* 1910. From left to right are: (standing) Minona Brannen, Lonnie Brannen, Solomon Brannen, Mrs. Pearl Lanier Brannen, Julian Brannen (holding infant Annie Laurie Brannen), young Aulbert J. Brannen, James Gross Brannen, Lawton Brannen, Lester Brannen, Mrs. James Gross (Sula Rogers) Brannen, Irvin Brannen, Eula Brannen, Janie Brannen Anderson, young Verna Anderson, Charles Anderson, young Perman Anderson, Jensie Brannen, Mrs. Annie Brannen Banks, young Osborne Banks, and David C. Banks (holding Lonnie Banks); (seated) Mrs. Sarah Hodges Brannen and Mrs. Juliann DeLoach Rogers, mothers of Mr. and Mrs. Brannen.

Dr. and Mrs. Daniel N. Nichols and their family were photographed in the Nichols cemetery near Portal, *c.* 1900. Dr. Nichols stands with his fourth wife at far right. The identically marked graves were monuments to Dr. Nichols's first three wives.

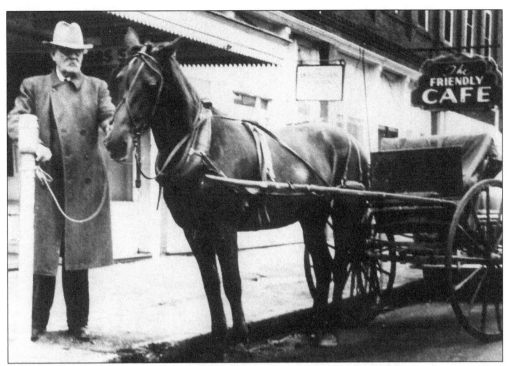

Colonel Albert Deal, noted Bulloch attorney, "parked" his horse and buggy near his law offices on North Main Street until his death in 1953. This special privilege was granted to him by an ordinance of the Statesboro City Council. While serving in the state legislature, he earned the nickname of "Square" Deal, a tribute to his honesty.

Shown here is the Bulloch County Fair Association, c. 1922. From left to right are: (front row) Walt Byrd, Brooks Sorrier, Lewis Akins, Hinton Booth, Dan Riggs, Joe Addison, and Barney Averitt; (back row) E.P. Josey, Darwin Franklin, Dave Turner, Lem Mikell, Grover Coleman, Frank Parker, and E.L. Poindexter.

In 1955, Miss Sarah Hall had the distinction of becoming the first woman to serve on a jury in Bulloch County. The director of Family and Children's Services, Miss Sarah was a highly regarded leader in civic and community affairs.

Members of Statesboro's Jewish community celebrated the Seder meal in the early 1950s. Since the beginning of Statesboro, Jewish citizens have been a vital part of the economic and cultural life of the community. Represented in the photograph are the families Rosenberg, Rosengart, Seligman, Minkovitz, Haimovitz, Levine, and Moses.

A bull session in the mule barn of Buggy and Wagon Company at the corner of Siebald and Courtland was captured in this c. 1949 photograph. From left to right are: Josh J. Zetterower, Police Chief Henry Anderson, First District Congressman Prince Preston, Josh Hagan, and veterinarian H.F. Hook.

In 1951, all segments of the Statesboro community met to prepare material for the All American Cities Contest scrapbook, sponsored by the Georgia Power Company. Mayor J. Gilbert Cone is at the far right. In the center foreground is Paul Carroll, dean of Georgia Teachers College. In the upper left are Henry McCormick and Kermit Carr.

Aaron Munlin was ordained to preach on December 7, 1878, by the Nevils Creek Primitive Baptist Church, the oldest church in Bulloch County. The former slave was often called upon to speak in homes and churches in both the white and black community. He organized the Banks Creek Primitive Baptist Church in 1879.

Mr. and Mrs. H.W.B. Smith Sr. celebrated their fiftieth wedding anniversary on October 14, 1958. The couple were noted educators and leaders in Bulloch's black community. Mr. Smith taught school for more than fifty-five years. He lived to be 106 years old. His wife, Mrs. Amanda Love Smith, taught school for over forty years. After retirement, she established the first kindergarten for black children in the county.

The Statesboro Regional Library began its traveling library in the early 1940s. This was the first bookmobile to serve a regional library system in the state of Georgia. Here, the truck delivers books and materials for students at the Statesboro Grammar School in 1946.

In 1959 this most up-to-date version of the bookmobile was featured at the American Library Association convention in Cincinnati, Ohio. The library building in the background was built in 1949. The library of 1997 is located on South Main Street at the same address.

In this view of East Main Street looking west, c. 1948, note the large oak tree on the Court House Square in right background, the streetlight on the right, and the advertisement for the newly air-conditioned Georgia Theatre. The theatre was known to locals as "the new show."

The old State Theatre is shown in its last days in this photo of 1963. Nicknamed the "old show," it was located on the south side of West Main, next door to Lonnie Griner's Farmer's Hardware Store. The alcove housed the box office and a refreshment stand. At times it was used as an exhibition area for touring spectacles, such as the bullet-riddled car of Bonnie and Clyde and the personal vehicle of Adolf Hitler.

Six

Enduring Moments

A typical Bulloch County farm was a "four-horse farm" of about 100 acres. In this c. 1900 photograph, on the left is an unidentified young farmer with his wife and child in the buggy. It was not unusual for mothers and children to assist with chores both at home and in the fields. Also pictured are the farmer's tenants, mules, wagons, and hound dog.

The rural mailman, Jake Daughtry, served residents in the Portal area in 1903. At the time, three rural mail routes originated in Statesboro. Each carrier began in the early morning and would cover a distance of about 30 miles, returning in the afternoon.

Friends posed for the camera on a leisurely Sunday afternoon in the Macedonia community in the early 1900s.

This is a wedding picture of David Callaway Banks and his wife Sarah Juliann "Annie" Brannen. They were married on December 23, 1906, in the Westside community at the home of the bride, the present-day Brannen-Banks house. Mr. and Mrs. Banks later lived in this house. Mrs. Banks was born, married, and later died in this house.

Bulloch Countians enjoyed the benefits of the mineral waters at Hot Springs, Arkansas. Here they pose for an ox cart ride. In 1908 their numbers included, from left to right (on the ox): J.A. "Lonnie" Brannen and Hiram Bonnette; (seated in the cart) John Suddath and James Gross "Jim Alex" Brannen; (standing on the back of the cart) Irvin A. Brannen, Pleasant B. Brannen, and John H. "Johnny" Brannen.

Here, "Son" Buie watches as Arthur Miller jokingly pretends to give Henry Miller a haircut in 1915.

In 1910, James Gross Brannen celebrated his fifty-sixth birthday with a big dinner spread on a long table in his backyard. Note the barn and stable on the far left and the cotton house in the center. Included in the photograph are his brothers, sisters, children, and their families. His home was in the Westside community.

Miss Lucy Olliff of Excelsior, Georgia, posed in one of the gowns of her trousseau in 1902, when she married Dr. J.T. Rogers, who practiced medicine in Statesboro for a number of years.

Sponsors for Camp # 1227 of Bulloch County's United Confederate Veterans assisted with Confederate Memorial Day activities in 1910. Each sponsor wore a dress of similar color and style. Miss Inez Williams is third from left. Inez Williams Park on North Main Street is named for her.

Here, the "Horseless Carriage" gets a push. This early 1900s photograph belongs to the Taylor DeLoach family, who lived in the Portal area.

In this photograph, S.W. Lewis Ford Company's mechanics and employees are shown with their wrecker in the 1930s. The vehicle's wheels have sturdy wooden spokes. The company was located on North Main, on what is now the site of the First Bulloch Bank.

Percy Averitt, at the wheel of his Buick automobile on the right, made a perfect score in the Savannah-to-Atlanta endurance race on November 8, 1909. With him is E.L. "Ed" Smith. In the other Buick on the left, driven by W.M. "Will" Hagins, is W.H. "Jack" Blitch, owner of the car. Behind them are Charles E. Cone and W.L. Hall in the rear seat.

Edward Perkins Gould (standing) and Elder Lee Gould enjoyed experimenting with an Excelsior motorcycle around 1915. This new machine combined the ambience of horseback riding with the efficiency of the automobile.

"The hurried-er I go, the behind-er I get." Hal Stewart clowned on his mule at his farm on Old River Road in Macedonia community, *c.* 1925.

Here, two men unload a crated casket from a dray wagon in an alley behind one of downtown Statesboro's funeral parlors, *c.* 1920.

Crowds gathered for a pond fishing at the lake at Roberts Mill (old Rigdon Mill) on Lake View road about 3 miles north of Statesboro in this *c.* 1920 photograph. This was the site of the Lake View Country Club. There were facilities for fishing, picnics, and dancing.

These men are seining for fish at a local pond in the 1950s.

This homemaker is using one of the first gas stoves in Bulloch County. The photograph is from the collection of Jeanette DeLoach Brinson.

A group of children gathered in front of Rawls Hardware Store around 1918. Mr. George Rawls sold many items which made house work easier, including the latest in wood-burning kitchen stoves. Note that downtown sidewalks then featured attractive hexagonal paving stones.

In 1917, Bob Miller and his wife, Gertrude Hagan Miller, were photographed at their home near Old River Road. The farm presently belongs to Mrs. Stothard Deal.

The Hagin sisters, Ida and Ada, picked pears in the family orchard in the early 1900s. The typical Bulloch County farm had a variety of fruit trees—pears, apples, peaches, and figs. The family lived in the Hagin District near Mill Ray.

Blind Willie McTell (1898–1959) called Statesboro home. He was an accomplished musician and writer of blues songs. Critics regard him as a master of the twelve-string guitar. McTell's most famous song, "Statesboro Blues," was popularized around 1970 by the Allman Brothers Band from Macon, Georgia.

Shown here are the grandchildren of Mrs. Hagar Hall. Mrs. Hall lived in the Hagin District in 1905. She was the mother of twelve children. Mrs. Hall and her family lived near the home of Dr. I.S.L. Miller, whose niece, Annie Darsey Burns, took this and the following photograph.

This is the daughter and granddaughter of Mrs. Hagar Hall of the Hagin District.

Here, a woman stands beside a well in rural Bulloch County. Before electricity was introduced in the 1940s, people depended upon this traditional method of gathering water. The rope passed through a pulley (called a tickle), as it raised or lowered the bucket deep into the well. This woman, like most rural folk, was accustomed to drawing many buckets of water daily for drinking, cooking, washing, and bathing.

Baby Kenneth Smith, surrounded by pullets, posed for this 1927 photograph which was taken in the family's chicken yard.

Buster Miller got around the farm in his wagon pulled by a family pet, "Old Bill." As an adult, Buster became an active and successful farmer in the Macedonia community.

Josh Smith Jr. (left) with his brother, Harold Smith, carved boats from cucumbers around 1925. Wading in the branch, they are floating their boats in the cool waters, after picking a lard bucket full of tomatoes.

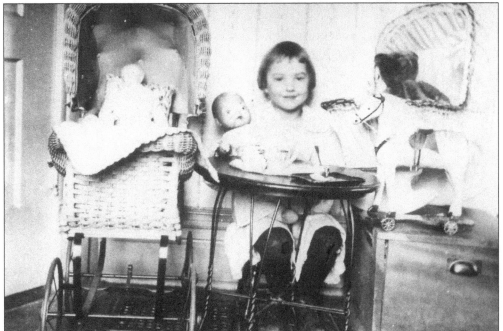

Jeanette DeLoach sits at her tea table and prepares a party for her collection of dolls and toy animals, in this photograph, c. 1920.

On April 1, 1908, a gentleman enjoyed the company of two young ladies at a local mill pond. The mirror-like surface of the pond reflects scenery that is familiar to all who know and love Bulloch County's natural beauty.

Mr. and Mrs. Will Kennedy posed at the picture booth for a souvenir of their Sunday excursion to Tybee Beach around 1905. Most travelers from Bulloch County took the train to Savannah, then took the streetcar or walked to the Tybee railroad station. The railroad was the only means of land transportation to the island. After spending a day of bathing and picnicking, the travelers returned home in the evening.

Sue Nell, daughter of Mr. and Mrs. Frank Smith, is shown at the water shelf on the back porch of her parent's rural home on Lakeview Road in 1932. In the center of the picture is a water faucet over a bucket. The china washbasin and a bar of soap were usual items on the shelf. After working in the fields, family members would wash their faces, hands, and feet at the back steps before entering the home.

In this c. 1920 photograph, Mamie Miller, daughter of Frank Miller, shows off her prized cow in the Hagin District.

Devastation and death: During the night of April 25, 1929, tornadoes hit Bulloch and surrounding counties and brought ruin to the citizens. Three tornadoes struck within several hours. Thirty-one people lost their lives, and sixty-four were seriously injured. The most serious devastation occurred on a straight path through Bulloch County from the upper edge of Candler County to Oliver in Screven County. This site is near Upper Lotts Creek Church.

This photograph shows the horrible ruins of a house struck by the tornado of 1929 in the Macedonia community.

In 1925. members of the Statesboro Gun Club enjoyed target shooting, including skeet and trap. Shown are twenty-two men who were among Statesboro's leading citizens. In the background is a sheltered grandstand for spectators. The club was located near the intersection of Highway 80 and North Zetterower Avenue.

During the fall at the beginning of deer season, hundreds of sportsmen engage in the ancient rituals of the hunt. Here, George Franklin makes Stothard Deal pay the price for missing an easy shot: Mr. Franklin cuts off a piece of Mr. Deal's shirt tail. Many hunting lodges decorate their walls with shirt tails from unlucky hunters.

"Miss Mattie," or Martha Brannen (Mrs. Gene) Bohler, shown here at age 88, demonstrated the art of spinning cotton thread during Bulloch County's Sesquicentennial celebration in December 1946.

The Statesboro Riding Club was photographed on a Sunday afternoon trek in the 1950s. Recognized among the riders are Lannie Simmons, Jessie O. Johnston, and Joe Johnston. In the center foreground is Charley P. Olliff Sr.

America W. (Mrs. Z.T.) DeLoach, affectionately known as "Miss Opie," celebrated Christmas at home in Portal around 1938. The decorations on the tree are typical of the time. The tall cedar is profusely decorated with icicles, ropes of garland, blown glass ornaments, and wreaths.

Here, Statesboro's semi-professional baseball team, the Pilots, are shown *c.* 1953 with manager J.C. "Jake" Hines (back row, extreme right) and batboys at front who are, from left to right, Jim Hines, Danny Bray, and Ashley Tyson. The baseball stadium, with covered bleachers, was located on the property of the Statesboro Airport. Hence the name, the "Pilots."

In 1948, the Cotillion Dance Club held their masquerade party and dance in the new clubhouse of the Forest Heights Country Club.

In a parade featuring bands, floats, and open convertibles, the city honored the tobacco harvest in the 1950s. The photographer, located on a stand on the Court House Square, captured the western side of the first block of North Main Street. Beautiful girls sit among sheets of tobacco which decorate the float sponsored by Brannen's Tobacco Warehouses.

A typical summer afternoon at the Statesboro Recreation Center Swimming Pool on South Zetterower Avenue, shortly after the facility opened on June 1, 1949, was captured here. Note the spectators lining the fence, the tobacco warehouse in the left background, and the absence of any commercial developments near the pool.

The Hula-Hoop craze swept through Statesboro in 1955. A contest sponsored by the Saturday morning Kiddie Show at radio station WWNS attracted many participants. The event took place on the front lawn of the station as part of a live broadcast.

In 1936 Sam Rosenberg moved from Portal to Statesboro to open a clothing store. Three generations of the family continued to operate the store until 1994. The store was located on South Main Street, at the corner of West Vine Street. Sam's son, Reuben, operated the store during most of its years of service. Here Reuben is shown with his daughter, Marilyn, in the 1960s.

Every spring, hundreds of children and their parents as well as senior citizens avidly participated in the annual fishing rodeo at Robbins Lake. The rodeo was sponsored by the Robbins Packing Company. From left to right are: Paul Humphrey, Mrs. Ruth Coursey, Robbie Humphrey, Gwenn Coursey, Cathy Brown, Frank Simmons III, Debra Coursey, and Wayne Hagan.

The Bulloch Four quartet began in 1946 as a group of friends who liked to sing. By the early 1950s they had become one of the most popular gospel quartets in southeast Georgia. From left to right are: Lewis Hursey at the piano, Christine Chandler (alto), Carl Bishop (bass), Otis Hollingsworth (baritone), and Bernard Banks (lead tenor).

In 1953, high school students danced the "Bunny Hop" at the Recreation Center on Fair Road. From left to right are: Ann Cason, Jane Richardson, Pat Alderman, Linda Bean, Guy McLendon, Patricia Lanier, unknown, Lynn Smith, Frederick Dyer, and John Lightfoot.

Acknowledgments

This volume would not exist without the assistance of a number of generous and helpful individuals. We are grateful that dozens of citizens shared treasured images from their families' collections. Especially we want to acknowledge Leodel and G.C. Coleman, former editors of the *Bulloch Herald* and *Statesboro Herald*, who donated their large and valuable collection of photographs to the Statesboro Regional Library. Other major sources include the following: the collection of post cards and historic photographs of Smith C. Banks; Ed Abercrombie's priceless "Vanishing Bulloch" photo project for the Bulloch County Historical Society; the Bulloch County Bicentennial Committee's exhibit at the Georgia Southern University Museum; the Department of Special Collections at the Henderson Library of Georgia Southern University, and especially our mentor, the indefatigable Dr. Kemp Mabry, executive vice president of the Bulloch County Historical Society. C. Bruce Miller generously loaned many photographs from his private collection and skillfully used computer technology to restore and enhance a number of historic photographs. Dr. Dan Good provided details for the map which Brad Higdon prepared for the Bulloch County bicentennial exhibit. Suzanne Oliver and Frank Fortune, expert and patient photographers, helped us meet our deadlines. We have consulted many publications of our state and local history. We wish to acknowledge and recommend *A Century of Progress* (1966), and *Spirit of the People* (1996), both published by the local newspaper, *The Statesboro Herald*. We also are indebted to two volumes of local history by the late Dorothy Brannen: *Early Churches of Bulloch County* (1983) and *Life in Old Bulloch: The Story of a Wiregrass County in Georgia* (1992). We have made every effort to identify each individual in the photographs, but many remain unidentified. Readers who can provide identifications are encouraged to notify the authors. Likewise, we will appreciate all who are kind enough to offer corrections.

Delma E. Presley and Smith C. Banks

From left to right in this photograph are Smith Callaway Banks, Kemp Mabry, Delma E. Presley, and Suzanne Oliver.

CPSIA information can be obtained
at www.ICGtesting.com
Printed in the USA
BVHW011109141119
563831BV00013B/148/P